6/12

TODAY'S ★★★ MARINE ★★★★★★ HEROES

by Michael Sandler

Consultant: Fred Pushies
U.S. SOF Adviser

BEARPORT
PUBLISHING

New York, New York

Credits

Cover and Title Page, © Joe Raedle/Getty Images and © Tyler Stableford/The Image Bank/Getty Images; 4, © AP Photo/Chao Soi Cheong; 5, © U.S. Air Force/Tech Sgt. Cedric H. Rudisill; 6, © LCpl. Samuel Bard Valliere/ DOD/ZUMA Press/Newscom; 7, © Dave Martin/AFP/Newscom; 8T, © U.S. Marine Corps; 8B, © Franco Pagetti/ VII/Corbis; 9, © U.S. Marine Corps/Lance Cpl. Jeremy W. Ferguson; 10, © Lucian Read; 11, © Lucian Read; 12, © Lucian Read; 13L, © U.S. Marine Corps/Sgt. Luis R. Agostini; 13R, © Charlie Neuman/San Diego Union-Tribune/ Zuma Press/Newscom; 14T, © Steven Barston; 14B, © U.S. Air Force/Tech Sgt. William Greer; 15, © U.S. Marine Corps/LtCol Mark A. Olson, IMEF Information Operations Officer; 16, © Mujahed Mohammed/AFP/ Getty Images/Newscom; 17, © Carrie Devorah/WENN.com/Newscom; 18T, Courtesy of Vernice "FlyGirl" Armour; 18B, © Science Faction/SuperStock; 19, Courtesy of Vernice "FlyGirl" Armour; 20T, © U.S. Marine Corps/Pfc. Michael T. Gams; 20B, © Science Faction/SuperStock; 21, © U.S. Marine Corps/Lance Cpl. Kelsey J. Green; 22T, © U.S. Marine Corps/Courtesy of Dakota Meyer; 22B, © Military.com; 23L, © U.S. Marine Corps/ Lance Cpl. David Rogers; 23R, © U.S. Marine Corps/Lance Cpl. Dale Jeon; 24, © U.S. Marine Corps/Courtesy of Dakota Meyer; 25, © Jason Reed/Reuters/Newscom; 26T, © U.S. Navy; 26B, © Toby Morris Photo/Zuma Press/ Newscom; 27, © DoD photo by Cherie A. Thurlby; 28T, © U.S. Marine Corps/Lance Cpl. Alesha R. Guard; 28B, © U.S. Marine Corps/Cpl. Katherine Keleher; 29, Photo by Jeff Schogol. Used with permission from Stars and Stripes. ©2010, 2011 Stars and Stripes; 31, © Keith McIntyre/Shutterstock.

Publisher: Kenn Goin
Senior Editor: Lisa Wiseman
Creative Director: Spencer Brinker
Design: Dawn Beard Creative
Photo Researcher: Picture Perfect Professionals, LLC

Library of Congress Cataloging-in-Publication Data

Sandler, Michael, 1965–
    Today's Marine heroes / by Michael Sandler ; consultant, Fred Pushies.
        p. cm. — (Acts of courage: inside America's military)
    Includes bibliographical references and index.
    Audience: Ages 7-12.
    ISBN-13: 978-1-61772-444-2 (library binding)
    ISBN-10: 1-61772-444-0 (library binding)
    1. United States. Marine Corps—Biography—Juvenile literature. 2. Iraq War, 2003—Biography—Juvenile literature. 3. Afghan War, 2001—Juvenile literature. I. Pushies, Fred J., 1952– II. Title.
    VE24.S28 2012
    956.7044'345092273—dc23
                          2011044374

For more information, write to Bearport Publishing Company, Inc., 45 West 21st Street, Suite 3B, New York, New York 10010. Printed in the United States of America.

10 9 8 7 6 5 4 3 2 1

★★★ Contents ★★★

A Tragic Day

September 11, 2001, began as a beautiful, clear day in New York City. However, at 8:46 that morning everything changed. An airplane full of people slammed into the North Tower of the World Trade Center. Less than 20 minutes later, a second plane crashed into the South Tower. Smoke poured from the massive buildings and flames shot out of the top floors.

The North and South Towers after being hit by the planes on September 11, 2001

The North and South Towers of the World Trade Center were called the twin towers.

The same morning, a plane flew into the **Pentagon** in Virginia and another one crashed into a field in Pennsylvania. The United States learned later that day that the four planes had been **hijacked** by members of a **terrorist group** called **Al Qaeda**. In all, nearly 3,000 people died. Al Qaeda's leader, Osama bin Laden, had organized the attack on the United States from his base in Afghanistan. Leaders in the United States decided the camps where Al Qaeda trained its soldiers needed to be destroyed. So in October 2001, the U.S. government sent **troops** to Afghanistan.

The Pentagon after being attacked on September 11, 2001

In War and Peace

The United States' war against terrorism expanded in 2003, when some government officials claimed that Saddam Hussein, the ruler of Iraq, was trying to build dangerous weapons, including **nuclear** ones. They feared he would use them against the United States and other countries. To stop him, the United States sent military troops to invade Iraq on March 20, 2003. Though the weapons were never found, the United States and its **allies** did remove Saddam Hussein from power.

Marines in Iraq

The Marine Corps is a part of the military that carries out missions on land and in the sea and air. The Marines have played a large part in America's wars in Afghanistan and Iraq. The red parts of this map show where some of the events in this book took place.

Thousands of brave men and women served in Afghanistan and Iraq in the years following the attack on the United States on September 11, 2001. This book recounts some of the acts of courage by U.S. Marines who fought in these wars. The bravery and **selflessness** they have shown in fighting for their country is the very definition of *hero*.

Marines not only fight in wars. They perform other important tasks, such as guarding American **embassies** in different countries and helping people when **natural disasters** strike.

Trapped in Fallujah

Brad Kasal

Rank:	First Sergeant (Later promoted to Sergeant Major)
Hometown:	Afton, Iowa
Conflict:	Iraq War
Date:	November 13, 2004
Honor:	Navy Cross

Some people are born to be Marines. First Sergeant (Sgt.) Brad Kasal is one of them. "I always wanted to be a Marine, to see the world and make a difference," he said. By November 2004, First Sgt. Kasal had served as a Marine for 20 years. That month, he took part in Operation Phantom Fury, fighting in the Iraqi city of Fallujah.

Operation Phantom Fury was a U.S. attack on **insurgents** in the town of Fallujah, about 50 miles (80 km) west of Baghdad, Iraq's capital. Marines went through the city street by street, searching for enemy fighters.

During the mission, First Sgt. Kasal spotted Marine Sgt. Christopher Pruitt coming out of a house, looking dazed and bleeding from his wrist and leg. Weaponless, Sgt. Pruitt was an easy target for enemy fighters.

Quickly, First Sgt. Kasal grabbed the injured Marine and dragged him to safety. That was when Sgt. Pruitt told him that there were three other wounded Marines inside the house. "I knew that they were dead if we left them in that building," First Sgt. Kasal said later.

Marines on the streets of Fallujah in November 2004

Enemy in the Darkness

As soon as First Sgt. Kasal heard about the wounded men trapped inside the house, he sprang into action. Along with other Marines who were **patrolling** the street, he raced into the house. Once inside, First Sgt. Kasal and Private First Class (Pfc.) Alex Nicoll carefully opened the door to a tiny dark room. An enemy fighter, holding a powerful gun called an AK-47, was on the other side. "Bad guy," yelled First Sgt. Kasal. A burst of bullets flew out of the enemy's machine gun, narrowly missing the two Marines. First Sgt. Kasal fired back, hitting the insurgent.

First Sgt. Kasal (left) and the other Marines waiting to enter a room in the house in Fallujah

The danger wasn't over, though. More enemy fighters were hiding behind the two Marines. They started shooting, spraying them with bullets and wounding both men. Would First Sgt. Kasal and Pfc. Nicoll make it out of the house alive?

After being shot by the hidden enemy fighters, First Sgt. Kasal was able to move Pfc. Nicoll inside the tiny room, where he treated the injured Marine's wounds. Each soldier was carrying only one emergency bandage. First. Sgt. Kasal ignored his own wounds and used both bandages to help Pfc. Nicoll.

The Marines make their way inside the room.

A Human Shield

Just when they thought the situation couldn't get any worse, First Sgt. Kasal heard the sound of a **hand grenade** rolling toward him! With no time to swat it away, he made a choice—to protect his **comrade** rather than himself. He rolled on top of Pfc. Nicoll, using his body as a shield. The grenade blew up, wounding First Sgt. Kasal in the back, shoulders, and legs. Incredibly, through all the pain, he stayed **conscious**. He kept guard over Pfc. Nicoll, trying to keep him from bleeding to death from the serious bullet wounds in his leg. Soon, another group of Marines entered the house, held off the enemy fighters, and rescued First Sgt. Kasal and Pfc. Nicoll.

First Sgt. Kasal (center) being carried out of the house

First Sgt. Kasal's injuries were severe, and his recovery took months. Still, he never regrets the choices he made to try to help his fellow Marines in Fallujah. "I'd do it a thousand times over, because I love the Marines," he said.

The Navy Cross

For his heroic actions, First Sgt. Brad Kasal was awarded the Navy Cross in 2006. This is the second-highest honor a Marine can receive.

Before being rescued, First Sgt. Kasal stayed alert and was able to help Pfc. Nicoll despite losing nearly 60 percent of his blood. Pfc. Nicoll lost his leg but survived. He would certainly have died without First Sgt. Kasal's heroic actions.

Terror in Tarmiya

Marco Martinez

Rank:	Corporal (Later promoted to Sergeant)
Hometown:	Albuquerque, New Mexico
Conflict:	Iraq War
Date:	April 12, 2003
Honor:	Navy Cross

Like First Sgt. Kasal, Corporal (Cpl.) Marco Martinez saved a fellow Marine from death with his heroic actions. In April 2003, Cpl. Martinez and his **platoon** were on a **scouting mission** in Tarmiya, a town located about 18 miles (29 km) north of Baghdad.

A street scene in Tarmiya, Iraq

As a teenager growing up in New Mexico, Marco Martinez got into trouble with gangs and crime. He joined the Marines and believes this helped turn his life around. "All I ever am, or will become, I owe to my beloved Corps," he says.

"As soon as we got into the area you felt this weird electricity in the air, like something was not right," Cpl. Martinez said. Indeed, something was very wrong. Enemy fighters were hidden in nearby houses. As the Marines stepped out of their armored vehicle, bullets and grenades flew through the air. One of the grenades wounded the platoon's leader. With their leader hurt, Cpl. Martinez had no choice but to take over the mission.

The type of armored vehicle Cpl. Martinez was traveling in is called an amtrack. These can carry Marines both on land and through water.

Saving a Soldier

With Cpl. Martinez leading the way, the platoon raced forward. They fired, forcing the enemy fighters to seek cover. However, the battle was still intense. Suddenly, one Marine was shot and fell to the ground. He was too **exposed** for anyone to help him. Enemy fighters in a nearby house would shoot any Marine who tried.

It was then that Cpl. Martinez spotted a **rocket-propelled grenade launcher** that an enemy fighter had dropped on the ground. Cpl. Martinez had never used one before, but he didn't hesitate for a moment. "I picked it up, and in about 30 seconds I learned how to shoot it," he said later.

An enemy fighter with a rocket-propelled grenade launcher

Cpl. Martinez launched a grenade into the house. It stunned the enemy fighters, giving the Marines time to rescue their fallen comrade. Then Cpl. Martinez charged into the house alone, clearing the building of the enemies remaining inside. Through strong action, he turned a possibly disastrous mission into a victory!

In 2004, Cpl. Martinez was awarded the Navy Cross for his heroic actions. He became the first Hispanic American to receive that award since the Vietnam War (1957–1975).

In 2010, Sgt. Marco Martinez (right) received the Paul Ray Smith Award from the American Veteran's Center for his heroism in the Iraq War.

Hero in a Helicopter

Vernice Armour

Rank: Captain

Hometown: Memphis, Tennessee

Conflict: Iraq War

Date: August 2004

Honor: Air Medal with a Combat "V" and the Global War on Terrorism Service Medal

While Marines fought on the ground in Iraq, Captain (Capt.) Vernice Armour supported them from the air. She flew an AH-1W Super Cobra attack helicopter that could fire down at enemy troops. Often, however, her helicopter came under attack. As a pilot her job was risky, but taking risks could save lives. "I'm there to protect men and women on the ground," she said.

Capt. Vernice Armour is not only the first African American female to fly a plane or helicopter for the Marine Corps; she is also the first African American female combat pilot in the U.S. military.

While serving in Iraq, Capt. Armour piloted the Super Cobra attack helicopter, shown here.

On one mission Capt. Armour helped out a group of Marines trapped in a cemetery. Enemy fighters were firing **mortars** at them from a nearby building. From high in the air, Capt. Armour's crew was able to identify the building. They launched rockets and a missile, destroying the enemies' guns and allowing the trapped Marines to escape.

A few months later, Capt. Armour met a Marine who was talking about being trapped in a battle. It was the battle during which the Marines had been trapped in the cemetery. When he realized that Capt. Armour was the one who had rescued them, he said, "Ma'am, you saved my life."

Capt. Vernice Armour earned several honors for her bravery and heroism in Iraq, including the Air Medal with a Combat "V" and the Global War on Terrorism Service Medal.

Unstoppable

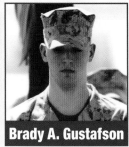

Brady A. Gustafson

Rank:	Lance Corporal
Hometown:	Eagan, Minnesota
Conflict:	War in Afghanistan
Date:	July 21, 2008
Honor:	Navy Cross

Lance Cpl. Brady Gustafson is another Marine who risked his life to save others. His act of **valor** took place in the village of Shewan, Afghanistan. When his four-vehicle **convoy** arrived in the quiet town, it was met with grenades and machine gun fire from **Taliban** fighters.

Lance Cpl. Gustafson fired back at them using the machine gun mounted in the **turret** of his **MRAP** vehicle. Suddenly, however, a rocket-propelled grenade flew into the MRAP and exploded. The grenade shattered Lance Cpl. Gustafson's right leg. "I looked down, and a lot of my right leg wasn't there," he said later.

turret

An MRAP

Incredibly, Lance Cpl. Gustafson didn't stop shooting. He fired more than 400 bullets at the Taliban fighters, keeping them away from the other Marines' vehicles. Finally, he allowed himself to be pulled away from the gun and was given badly needed first aid by fellow Marines. His actions helped give the Marines time to escape, which was all that mattered to Lance Cpl. Gustafson. "We didn't lose a single Marine," he said.

For his heroic actions, Lance Cpl. Gustafson (right) was awarded the Navy Cross on March 27, 2009.

The Marine driving Lance Cpl. Gustafson's MRAP was wounded and knocked **unconscious** when the attack began. The ten minutes that Lance Cpl. Gustafson spent shooting gave the driver time to regain consciousness and drive the Marines to safety.

Ambush in Ganjgal

Dakota Meyer

Rank:	Corporal (Later promoted to Sergeant)
Hometown:	Columbia, Kentucky
Conflict:	War in Afghanistan
Date:	September 8, 2009
Honor:	Medal of Honor

For American soldiers, any day in Afghanistan could be tough. Few, however, were tougher than the one faced by a group of Marines on September 8, 2009. The Marines were working with Afghan soldiers on an early-morning mission in the village of Ganjgal. Their job was to meet with village leaders and set up police patrols in the area.

Marines patrolling in the valley of Ganjgal

The United States is at war with members of the Taliban and Al Qaeda, not with the Afghan people. In fact, many members of the U.S. military help train Afghans as soldiers so they can protect their country and help the United States fight the insurgents.

Just before dawn, the Marines entered a **ravine** near the village. Two Marines, Cpl. Dakota Meyer and Staff Sgt. Juan Rodriguez-Chavez, stayed behind, waiting with their **Humvees**. Suddenly, more than 50 Taliban fighters **ambushed** the group in the ravine. Bullets and grenades came at the group from three sides. Capt. Ademola Fabayo, the leader of the mission, helped some of the soldiers escape. Still, many others remained trapped. Cpl. Meyer and Sgt. Rodriguez-Chavez could hear the battle from where they were. Even though they had been told not to enter the combat zone, they knew what they had to do. "We have to get in there," said Cpl. Meyer.

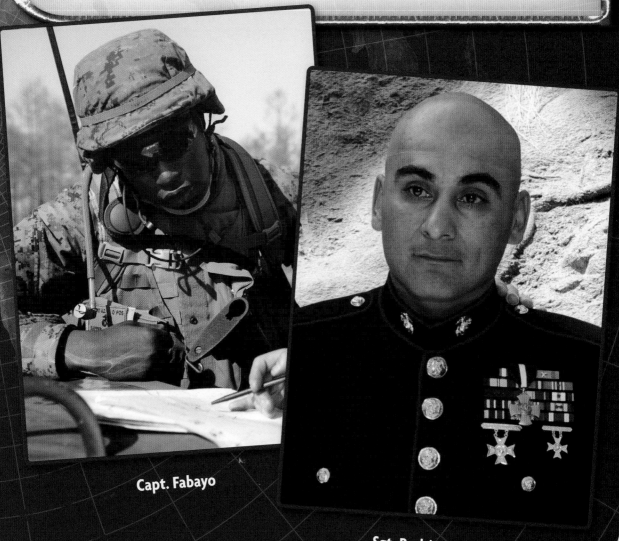

Capt. Fabayo

Sgt. Rodriguez-Chavez

Straight into Danger

Cpl. Meyer didn't think twice about heading into danger. "My best friends were in there getting shot at," he said later. The pair jumped into one of the Humvees, with Sgt. Rodriguez-Chavez at the wheel and Cpl. Meyer manning the gun mounted in the turret of the vehicle. They drove into the ravine as bullets and grenades flew at them. Whenever they spotted Marines or Afghan soldiers, Sgt. Rodriguez-Chavez slowed down. Then Cpl. Meyer jumped out to rescue them. Together, they saved dozens of men in four trips into the ravine.

Cpl. Meyer in Afghanistan

On one trip, Cpl. Meyer was wounded in the arm, but he wouldn't give up. Four Marines remained in the danger zone. It was impossible to get the Humvee close to them, so Cpl. Meyer jumped out and headed into the battleground on foot. Tragically, it was too late to save the four men. They had died in the attack. Cpl. Meyer refused to leave their fallen bodies in enemy hands, however. With help from some of the others, he brought their bodies out of the valley.

On September 15, 2011, Sgt. Dakota Meyer received the Medal of Honor for his courage. He is the first living Marine in 41 years to be awarded this medal, the nation's highest award for bravery. Both Sgt. Rodriguez-Chavez and Capt. Fabayo were honored with the Navy Cross on June 10, 2011.

Sgt. Dakota Meyer after receiving his Medal of Honor from President Barack Obama

The Greatest Sacrifice

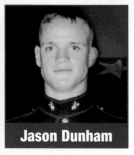

Jason Dunham

Rank: Corporal

Hometown: Scio, New York

Conflict: Iraq War

Date: April 14, 2004

Honor: Medal of Honor

Marines have bravely served in each of America's wars since 1775 and thousands have given their lives in battle. Cpl. Jason Dunham was one of those brave and selfless Marines who made the greatest **sacrifice** of all. Cpl. Dunham was on patrol near Karabilah, Iraq, when insurgents attacked some Marines. He and his men rushed to the area to help. They saw a group of cars beginning to drive away. Suspecting that these were the attackers, the Marines stopped the vehicles.

In Iraq, Marines often stop and inspect cars that seem suspicious to them.

Suddenly, a man jumped out of one of the cars and attacked Cpl. Dunham. When two other Marines rushed over to help, the attacker dropped a grenade on the ground! Without hesitating, Cpl. Dunham grabbed his helmet and threw it over the grenade. He held the helmet down with his body as the grenade exploded. Sadly, Cpl. Dunham's brave action killed him, but it saved the lives of two other Marines.

Cpl. Dunham's sacrifice is an example of extraordinary valor, the type for which Marines are known. In years to come, the Marines will continue to show this kind of bravery and be willing to take on any challenge—even when it means paying the ultimate price to serve their country.

On January 11, 2007, President George Bush presented the Medal of Honor to Jason's parents, Deb and Dan Dunham. Cpl. Dunham became the first Marine to receive the Medal of Honor since the Vietnam War (1957–1975). Cpl. Dunham's other awards included a Purple Heart and a Combat Action ribbon.

Only ten soldiers have received the Medal of Honor for their service during the wars in Afghanistan and Iraq.

More Marine Heroes

Here are a few more U.S. Marine heroes who have worked hard to serve their country.

First Lieutenant Rebecca M. Turpin

⭐ First Lieutenant Rebecca M. Turpin ⭐

First Lieutenant Rebecca M. Turpin showed her courage in Afghanistan on December 13, 2008. She led her platoon on a dangerous mission to deliver food, water, and other supplies to soldiers deep in the Afghan countryside. The road was littered with buried explosives, and First Lieutenant Turpin's convoy came under repeated attack by machine guns and grenades. She, however, kept her fellow Marines alive and was able to deliver the badly needed supplies. For her heroic actions she received the Navy and Marine Corps Commendation Medal with a Combat "V."

Cpl. Kimberly Burkett

⭐ Lance Cpl. Kimberly Burkett ⭐

Marines can't fight if their basic needs aren't met. That's why feeding Marines in the field is an important military job. At Camp Leatherneck in the Helmand province of Afghanistan, Marine food specialists, such as Lance Cpl. Kimberly Burkett, have an important job—working nonstop to keep soldiers well fed. Each day, 4,000 meals are served at the camp—that's over four million a year. Said one sergeant in the Marines, "If there weren't food service Marines, then nobody would be eating."

★ Master Gunnery Sgt. Charles Padilla ★

Master Gunnery Sgt. Charles Padilla helped his fellow Marines in an unusual way—by running across the country as part of a six-man team. Beginning in New York on September 10, 2010, Sgt. Padilla and his team braved rain and hail, and crossed deserts and mountain ranges in a 3,530-mile (5,681-km) race across America. The team's aim was to raise money for fellow Marines who were badly wounded in Iraq or Afghanistan. It took the team 64 days to reach Los Angeles, California.

**Master Gunnery Sgt. Charles Padilla (right)
runs with some members of his team.**

Glossary

allies (AL-eyez) friends or supporters

Al Qaeda (AHL KAY-duh) the terrorist group that was responsible for the September 11, 2001, attacks on the United States

ambushed (AM-busht) attacked suddenly by surprise

comrade (KOM-rad) a friend, companion, or fellow group member

conscious (KON-shuss) being awake, alert, and able to think

convoy (KON-voi) a group of military vehicles traveling together for safety

embassies (EM-buh-seez) buildings in foreign countries where ambassadors live and work

exposed (ek-SPOHZD) made open to possible attack

hand grenade (HAND gruh-NADE) a small bomb that is thrown by hand

hijacked (HYE-jackt) illegally took control of by force

Humvees (hum-VEEZ) jeep-like military vehicles that can move troops and travel over rough roads

insurgents (in-SUR-junts) people who fight against a lawful government or lawful leaders

mortars (MOR-turz) cannon-like weapons that fire shells

MRAP (EM-AHR-AY-PEE) stands for *Mine Resistant Ambush Protected*; a military vehicle that is designed to withstand roadside bombs and other kinds of attacks

natural disasters (NACH-ur-uhl duh-ZASS-turz) disasters such as earthquakes or tsunamis that are caused by nature rather than by people

nuclear (NOO-klee-ur) having to do with a dangerous type of energy that produces radiation

patrolling (puh-TROHL-ing) traveling around an area to keep it safe

Pentagon (PEN-tuh-gon) the five-sided building in Virginia that serves as the headquarters of the U.S. Department of Defense

platoon (pluh-TOON) a group of soldiers who live and train together

ravine (ruh-VEEN) a deep, narrow valley with steep sides

rocket-propelled grenade launcher (ROK-it-pruh-PELD gruh-NADE LAWNCH-ur) a weapon that is used to shoot a grenade a long distance

sacrifice (SAK-ruh-*fisse*) to give up something in order to help someone else

scouting mission (SKOUT-ing MISH-uhn) an important job or task that involves investigating an area to gather information

selflessness (SELF-less-ness) not thinking about one's self; putting the needs of other people first

Taliban (TAL-ah-ban) a military and political group that ruled Afghanistan from 1996 to 2001 and remains a strong force in the country

terrorist group (TER-ur-ist GROOP) people who use violence to get what they want

troops (TROOPS) groups of soldiers

turret (TUHR-it) a protected area on top of a vehicle from which a Marine can shoot at the enemy in any direction

unconscious (uhn-KON-shuhss) not awake; unable to think, hear, feel, or see

valor (VAL-ur) bravery or courage shown in battle

Bibliography

Larson, Major Chuck, ed. *Heroes Among Us: Firsthand Accounts of Combat from America's Most Decorated Warriors in Iraq and Afghanistan.* New York: New American Library (2008).

Marines Magazine

The Navy Times Magazine

The New York Times

Marines.com

Read More

Goldish, Meish. *Marine Corps: Civilian to Marine (Becoming a Soldier).* New York: Bearport (2010).

Mason, Paul. *Iraq (Countries Around the World).* Mankato, MN: Heinemann-Raintree (2011).

Sandler, Michael. *Marine Force Recon in Action (Special Ops).* New York: Bearport (2008).

Learn More Online

To learn more about today's Marine heroes, visit
www.bearportpublishing.com/ActsofCourage

Index

About the Author

Michael Sandler has written many children's nonfiction books. He lives in Brooklyn, New York, with fellow writer Sunita Apte and their two children, Laszlo and Asha. Michael is an avid traveler.